BOB MARLEY *In His Own Words*

n McCann

Bob Marley

"*Talking*"

BOB MARLEY *Talking*

First published © 1993 Omnibus Press
This edition Copyright © 2003 Omnibus Press
(A Division of Music Sales Limited)

Cover & book designed by Fresh Lemon.
Picture research by Dave Brolan & Sarah Bacon.

ISBN: 0.7119.9766.7
Order No: OP49379

Exclusive Distributors
Music Sales Limited, 8/9 Frith Street, London W1D 3JB, UK.

Music Sales Corporation,
257 Park Avenue South, New York, NY 10010, USA.

Macmillan Distribution Services,
53 Park West Drive, Derrimut, Vic 3030, Australia.

To the Music Trade only:
Music Sales Limited,
8/9 Frith Street, London W1D 3JB, UK.

Photo credits:
All Images 56 Hope Road Music / Adrian Boot.

Every effort has been made to trace the
copyright holders of the photographs in this book but one or two were unreachable.
We would be grateful if the photographers concerned would contact us.

Printed by Caligraving Ltd, Thetford, Norfolk.

A catalogue record for this book is available from the British Library.

Visit Omnibus Press on the web at www.omnibuspress.com

Introduction & Acknowledgements 6

Early Days 10

Friends & Associates 17

Records & Songs 25

Reggae 33

Music 39

Politics 45

Struggle 49

His Message 55

Rasta 59

Race 67

Jah 71

Africa & Repatriation 73

America 77

Business 81

Violence 85

Lifestyle 89

Women 95

Herb 97

Stardom 100

Media 103

Illness 105

Natural Mystic 107

CONTENTS

In compiling this book, it has again become apparent to me that Bob Marley really was a one-off.

While his words are frequently couched in a Jamaican ghetto dialect that has since, to a degree, been superseded by the tougher language of younger generations growing up in—arguably—an even harsher environment than he did, the thrust of Marley's thought remains piercing. No entertainer was ever asked the questions he was asked as a matter of course. When other stars are pressed on revolution or religion, they respond with platitudes or clichés. With Marley you always expected more, and usually got it. Even if he changed his ideas from time to time—as he did, like everyone else with an active mind—he always had "so much things to say".

Introduction

Some of them are on offer here. To Marley's credit, he rarely refused an interview. Most songwriters have little of interest to say while away from their guitar. You could probably get as many fascinating quotes from Bob Dylan, a figure with whom Marley has often been compared, except that Dylan wouldn't give you the quotes in the first place. Marley saw press interrogation as part of his job, and his duty—how else could the world comprehend Rastafari if he wasn't prepared to explain it? Even when the press got him entirely wrong, still he'd persist. Bob Marley was interested in being understood and in understanding, and I hope that this book will help in that quest a little. His eloquence is rare: even when, under the enormous pressure of being strife-torn Jamaica's number one hero, he's effectively saying "Look, I can't speak on this subject", still his opinion comes across.

A couple of points: I've tried to avoid too many 'mons' in the quotes, as everyone knows he means 'man' and spelling it to take account of his accent seems patronising. You wouldn't, after all, spell the same word in a Prince Charles speech as 'mern' unless you were being deliberately cynical. The quotes are littered with Jamaican patois, to create more is pointless. Likewise, a glossary of the dialect would be equally patronising: a couple of reads will make anything clear. Marley is not from Venus, after all. Just remember that 'fe' means 'for' or 'to' and you've virtually cracked it.

Marley was no angel, his was a tough life and he was a tough cookie with a wicked sense of humour to boot. Accept his quotes for what they are: whether you agree or disagree, he will stimulate. Doubtless, when confronted with the wrong writer, he would bullshit and deliberately say something provocative. Those quotes are here alongside his more serious moments. If you suspect that he is, after all these years, still pulling our legs in a few places here, then who the cap fits, let them wear it. Likewise, this isn't a Marley biography: there are several excellent biogs already, to which I am indebted, as the acknowledgements make clear. Rather, this book is intended as a companion-piece to his records and to the reams already written about him.

I promise you, the last thing you need is a book full of me pretending I was present at all moments of his life. The chapter headed 'Illness' is perhaps a little controversial, but I feel its presence is merited. It shows Marley facing up to the final challenge in his life of tribulation, melanoma, and coming to terms with impending death. I hope that a little of his bravery and implacable spirit comes through. Although it has been well over a decade since he died, his influence and music still rattle the windows around the world today.

As for reggae, it thrives without him, after a few introspective hiccups following his death. He is, of course, irreplaceable, but that doesn't trouble reggae. While it may never again offer a songwriter of his international credibility, in a way it doesn't need to. Reggae, Jamaica and the world have already had their Bob Marley. One is enough. To ask for two would be sheer greed.

INTRODUCTION

Many sincere thanks to the following people without whom this
book would not exist: Joan Baguley, Noel Hawks, Danny Kelly and *NME,*
Rob Partridge, Chris Charlesworth, Gaylene Martin. Also thanks to mum
and dad.

Big respect due to the following publications for the endless groundwork
on which I was gratefully able to draw: New Musical Express, The Face,
Sounds, Melody Maker, Echoes, Black Music, Oui, Blues & Soul, No Chains
Around My Feet, ZigZag, Time Out, The Times, Daily Mail, Daily Mirror,
The Jamaica Daily News, The Jamaican Weekly Gleaner, Rolling Stone,
Street Life, Crawdaddy, Sunday Express (Jamaica), Record Mirror,
The Guardian, The Best Of Rebel Music.

Acknowledgements

The following books have been invaluable:
Bob Marley, Soul Rebel-Natural Mystic
by Adrian Boot/Vivien Goldman *(Eel Pie/Hutchinson)*
Bob Marley by Stephen Davis *(Arthur Barker)*
Catch A Fire, The Life Of Bob Marley by Timothy White *(Omnibus Press)*
Jah Music by Sebastian Clarke *(HEB)*
Reggae Bloodlines by Stephen Davis & Peter Simon *(Anchor Press/
Doubleday)*
Reggae International by Stephen Davis & Peter Simon *(Thames & Hudson)*
Bob Marley by Cathy McKnight & John Tobler *(Star)*
Bob Marley, Reggae King Of The World
by Malika Lee Whitney & Dermott Hussey

Sincere thanks to the following writers: Chris Lane, Vivien Goldman,
Sebastian Clarke, Neil Spencer, Stephen Davis, Timothy White, Sheryl
Garratt, Penny Reel, Chris May, Cathy McKnight, John Tobler, Malika Lee
Whitney, Dermott Hussey, Carl Gayle, Roz Reines, Ray Coleman, Harry
Hawk, Keith Bourton, Paul Gambaccini, Colin Irwin, Kris Needs, Paolo
Hewitt, Karl Dallas, Jon Futrell, John Williams, Mike Phillips, Chris Salewicz,
Richard Grabel, Myles Palmer, Martin J Rowbotham, Scott Cohen.

Ian McCann, June 1992

Early Days

"Started out crying. Started out crying y'know. And then music becomes a part (of my life) because me grateful to Jah." 1973

"Me grew up in the country, in the woods, to the city, ya know? A place named St Ann's. That's the garden parish, they call it the 'Garden Parish', and now me grow in Kingston, from Barry Street, den to Oxford Street, to Regent Street, and then to Trenchtown. Me lived in Trenchtown from 1958 to 1961. Then all over." 1975

"(At school) the teacher say 'Who can write, write. Who can sing, sing.' So me sing." JUNE, 1975

"I don't really know (how I got started) but I know me mother was a singer first. Me mother is spiritual, like a gospel singer. She writes songs. I hear her singing first and then... I just love music, love it, grow with it." 1975

"I was a skinny child with a squeaky voice. So skinny! Skinny like a stringy bean!" 1978

"I find my mother (Cedella Booker) works for fifty shillings a week and on this she has to send me to school, buy me shoes and lunches." 1977

"Me saw dem have a little t'ing down at Queens (Theater, Kingston). So one night me go in and sing a tune. Me nuh remember what it was but me win a pound. The man tell me me must start sing. And me did." 1976

BOB MARLEY *Talking*

" As a youth I was always active, never lazy. I learnt a trade, welding, so dealing with those things is part of my thing. I enjoy dealing with parts, partwork, and I never really mind because I just did it as much as I wanted to do it. Anytime I felt fed-up, I didn't really look for a job. " JULY, 1979

" Me did sing in school and love singing, but when me really tek it seriously is when I go and learn a trade name welding. Desmond Dekker used to learn trade same place and we used to sing and him write songs. Then something happened to Desmond's eye, a little teeny piece of iron fly into it and him go doctor and have some days off. The days him have off him go check out Beverlys (record company) and him do a thing name 'Honour Your Mother And Father' which was a big hit in Jamaica. After that him just say come man and me go down there (Beverlys) and meet Jimmy Cliff and him get me audition and me record a song for Beverlys. It never really do nothing but it was a good song still name 'Judge Not'. " SEPTEMBER, 1975

" When I started singing, I couldn't play an instrument. We still have these musicians who play the instruments and are playing better music than we play today. But the guys who used to do the thing, it was a young thing growing. I can remember the first time when I hear a record when the thing was going to get popular, when Jamaican singers in Jamaica was gonna get popular like Wilfred Edwards and Owen Grey and Jimmy Cliff, Lord Tanamo. Plenty of them type a guys, during those times. And then it changed. The guys who used to, like

BOB'S MOTHER CEDELLA BOOKER

NEVILLE 'BUNNY WAILER' LIVINGSTON

me, go to a studio, and you come to me and say, 'You can play?' and me say, 'Yes' and you will want the opportunity. Because there is no work, although you can get work, but who want to work for £5 a week. Not at that time. Music was the t'ing.** 1975

Well, I never really take it (guitar playing) seriously, see? Most times I just take up a guitar and I just play like ah, but I never really used to do no recordin'—until the musicians that was really playin' the music at that time, they get so ripped off that they would play no more. And so was getting no good music again. So we start playin' it ourselves. 1975

We used to sing in the back of Trench Town and rehearse plenty until The Drifters came on 'pon the scene and me love group singing so me just say, well me 'ave fe go look a group.
SEPTEMBER, 1975

My greatest influence (in early times) was The Drifters—'Magic Moment', 'Please Stay', those things. So I figured I should get a group together. FEBRUARY, 1973

We go out now and me find some little youths round me a sing. Then Bunny (Livingston) so we form a group. We go look fe Peter (Tosh). We see Peter 'pon the street, me never even know him fe talk to. We hear him a play him guitar and sing and we figure say, yes, him sound strong. So we get together and form a group plus two girls and a next little youth called Junior Braithwaite. So we go up to Coxsone (CS Dodd, producer for, and owner of, Studio One record label) and we do 'Simmer Down'. We go on until we had to leggo the two girls. Them was good in recording but go 'pon stage and mek a mistake... but dem sisters did great, could sing high. SEPTEMBER, 1975

EARLY DAYS

"Name Wailers come from the Bible. There's plenty places you meet up with weeping and wailing. Children always wail y'know, cryin' out for justice and all that." 1974

"We call ourselves de Wailers because we started out cryin'." 1972

"We did... rude boy songs. That rude boy business was bad, bad music. Only them shouldn't have said rude boy, them should've said Rasta. But in them times me didn't know Rasta. Something was going on, you felt it and didn't know if you were bad bad or good good—then I understood— it's good, you're good, it's Rasta." JULY, 1979

Did you play a lot of gigs in the early days?

"Not a lot, just Christmas and Easter morning, we'd be up there at the Carib Theater (a Kingston cinema). But we was always the underground, always the rebels. We come from Trenchtown. So you'd hear about Byron Lee (MOR Jamaican bandleader-producer) and all that society business, but we come from down (town) so, named Wailers from Trenchtown." JULY, 1979

"Do you like Two-Tone? Some of it sound good man. When I hear it, it take me back to some rass days. I'll tell you, them were the days of The Skatalites—them just a come with some musician named Don Drummond, and another guy who could tear it up on the tenor sax, Roland Alphonso, a rass player man! Him still play too, even though something happen to him, a stroke down one side. But what a player though." SEPTEMBER, 1980

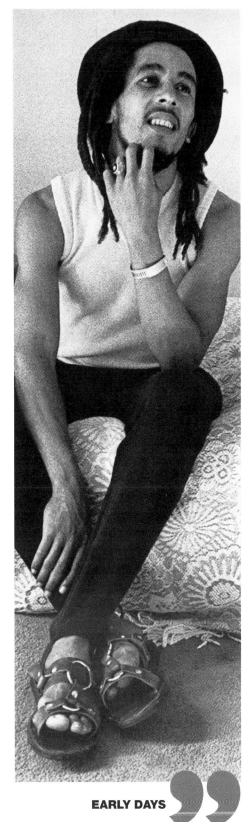

"Yah see, my people was always amongst bars. You have jukebox and you always have music going on. I remember we used to have plenty plenty music. And one time me saw a show down here (Kingston) with Brook Benton and Dinah Washington. Like they all show up: Nat King Cole, Billy Eckstine, y'know. Even Frank Sinatra and Sammy Davis in a certain period when I was living on Oxford Street. But when I was living in Barry Street I used to hear things like 'Jim Dandy To The Rescue', 'Bony Maronie', 'What Am I Living' For', 'Don't Break Your Promise To Me'. Heavy music. Then we go to Regent Street now, and me hear Brook Benton and some work with a guy named Danny Ray. But Fats Domino and Ricky Nelson and Elvis Presley and whole heap of likkle other music come on strong. Then we go to Second Street and start listening to jazz. Except me couldn't understand it. After a while me get to understand it and me meet Joe Higgs and Seeco Patterson who schooled me. After a while I smoked some ganja, some herb, and then I understood jazz. I tried to get into the mood where the moon is blue and understand the feelings expressed." 1975

"One year (1966) we make hits like 'Put It On', 'Rude Boy', 'Rule Them Rudie', 'I'm Still Waiting'. And we expect to get some money, for this is Christmas. Then the guy (Coxsone Dodd) give we 60 after we mek so much hits. So me just leggo and go live with me mother in America. Over there me find the music still in me, singing and writing some good tune like 'Bend Down Low'. We come back to Jamaica and do 'Bend Down Low' which was a hit and them rob we out of it again. We come back with 'Nice Time' but man is all robbery. Rob you down to nothin'." SEPTEMBER, 1975

"I thought I wasn't going to work for anyone again, so we split from Coxsone (Dodd) to form Wail'n'Soul (1967). But I don't know anything about business and I got caught again. 'Bend Down Low' was number one in Jamaica but they were pressing and selling it (in) a black market type of business." 1976

"We fight hard, man (to make Wail'n'Soul a success). But when Christmas come and we go to collect money, the man say the (record) stamper mosh (destroyed) and alla that." 1976

"The politics get hot and the city get hot so I was in the country planting corn (1968). Johnny Nash and his manager came down to me to write songs for them. They felt like I was finished with music. They didn't know I was only resting." 1976

Friends & Associates

Joe Higgs
Marley's early mentor

❝Him, you know, is one heavy music man, Joe Higgs. I feel like him need a little more time fe love, him want a little more love. Joe good but him want a little bit more time fe get him things together.❞ SEPTEMBER, 1975

❝Joe Higgs helped me to understand that (jazz) music. He taught me many things.❞ 1975

Leslie Kong
Jamaican producer, who cut Marley's first two records, 'Judge Not' and 'Do You Still Love Me'.

❝I meet Leslie Kong at Federal. I was looking for a Count Boysie, and Desmond Dekker say I should check Leslie Kong. And dat man rude ! Tell me ta sing my song straight out, standing outside. Didn't have no guitar, rass-clot. Dat focker! Him take me inna room, past Chinamon and this guy Ken Khouri, who tek the money and put it inna pounch on ' im chest. No, Kong must pay for the studio time for me. So I sing and Kong pay me two ten pounds note and then push me out. When I say to him, 'What if it a hit?' him say, 'Coo pon', and say I'm trying to rax (wreck) the deal. Them bloodclot. Mon-a name-a Dowling make I sign the release form, them then push me out a studio, and I run home. First I wait for acetates, then I run home.❞ 1975

BOB MARLEY *Talking*

Peter Tosh
original Wailer

PETER TOSH

❝You not supposed to feel down over whatever happen to you. I mean, you supposed to use whatever happen to you as some type of upper, not a downer. Say if a brother say he don't wanna play no more music then you have a little time to work out what is to be, what must be. I feel Peter Tosh was want to have adventures himself. Him talented enough and mebbe him want something better than this.❞ JULY, 1975

Bunny Wailer
original Wailer

❝Bunny was like me bredda (brother) in them (early, 1964) times. Me used to live with him father. So we form a group.❞ SEPTEMBER, 1975

Junior Braithwaite
original Wailer

❝Man could sing, man. Him sing a tune name 'Hurts To Be Alone'... papa, phew! We see him in Chicago the other day. Him a write music and things but him did sick.❞ SEPTEMBER, 1975

❝Junior used to sing high. It's just nowadays that I'm beginning to realise that he sounded like one of The Jackson Five.❞ 1974

Aston and Carlton Barrett
Wailers' drum and bass

"Everybody have to stay root. Like Aston and Carlton Barrett, y'know. Ya cyaan (can't) return to the roots, you must be the roots. Guy think he can return to the roots when he was a leaf, he drop off and that how he return to the roots. We must be the roots."

MAY, 1977

WITH ASTON 'FAMILY MAN' BARRETT (LEFT)
AND CARLTON BARRETT

Split of the 'original Wailers'
1973-4

"Me really used to work hard you know, but if you in a group and you get tense... me no want say this but me little bit tense with The Wailers we have first time, Bunny and Peter. Is like them don't want understand me can't just play music fe Jamaica alone.

Can't learn that way. Me get the most of my learning when me travel and talk to other people. That was a kind of worry me have why me never so loose before. They can be a part of the group but me 'ave fe leave Jamaica certain time because of politics in the air. The influence from politicians we have is strong. Them love come to you and try get you, and me is a man no like turn down no-one. So me leave Jamaica.**"** JULY, 1975

Why was your last tour of England cancelled?

"Yeh... well, the thing was, some of the members of the group can't stand the cold." JULY, 1975

Al Anderson

"Why did you choose an American to play lead guitar? We really not deal with people in categories like if you come from Jamaica you have the right. Regardless of where you are on earth you have the right. I can't deal with the passport thing. To me him prove himself not an outsider because if him can play with us then him no outsider.**"** JULY, 1975

AL ANDERSON & JUNIOR MARVIN

"I'm meet Al in England while he was doing some overdub guitar. We talk a little and it's nice, ya know? So I ask him to come and play with the group. Him think about it for some time and then him decide he would do it. Boy, him great! Fuckin' good mon!" 1975

FRIENDS & ASSOCIATES

Johnny Nash

You wrote many songs for Johnny Nash. What do you think of him?

"He's a hard worker but he didn't know my music. I don't want to put him down, but reggae isn't really his bag. We knew of Johnny Nash in Jamaica before he arrived but we didn't love him that much. We appreciated him singing the kind of music he does—he was the first US artist to do reggae — but he isn't really our idol. That's Otis (Redding) or James Brown or (Wilson) Pickett, the people who work it more hard." 1973

"He's good. I like him." 1975

Taj Mahal

"We developed a kind of telepathic contact. He said he was going to do 'Slave Driver' so I went to meet him. He's good and he's strong and he's got a West Indian thing." 1975

Family

"I have a sister, ya know. My father was her father but she has a different mother. I knew about her since I was a youth, and alla time I search for her. Once time, when I was in my twenties, I find her. She was workin' in a dry cleaners in Kingston. I talked with her for just a few minutes and then we said goodbye, me thinking I was gonna see (her) again. But when I go back a few days later she is gone. I never found her again. It was a painful thing, not to know her." AUGUST, 1978

"I love Jamaica and I love the people but I have to move up and down the earth. My mother tell me God is the father for the fatherless. So where he sends me I must go. No man can tell me what to do. I have seven children and I would make a million tunes here and can't put my children in a room. I can't afford to make my children grow up like me. I love the brethren and I love the children but I can't afford to stay here and go to prison."

AUGUST, 1974

PART OF MARLEY FAMILY - JULIAN, STEVE, CEDELLA, RITA

FRIENDS & **ASSOCIATES**

Records & Songs

'Catch A Fire'

❝'Catch A Fire' was an introduction. Nobody know who Bob Marley & The Wailers was, at the same time maybe you have other group who people were more interested in at the time. It was for people get in and listen.❞ 1974

'Natty Dread'

❝The 'Natty Dread' album is, like one step more towards (for) reggae music. Better music, better lyric, it have a better feelin'. 'Catch A Fire' and 'Burnin'' have a good feelin' but 'Natty Dread' is improved.❞ 1974

'So Jah Seh'

❝So Jah seh, not one of my seed shall sit on the sidewalk and beg bread. What we really mean is progress. People a fe start live together. I don't know so much the big people, but the youth must get together.❞ 1974

'No Woman No Cry'

❝Me really love 'No Woman No Cry' because it mean so much to me, so much feeling me get from it. Really love it.❞ 1974

BOB MARLEY *Talking*

'Rastaman Vibration'

❝It comes nicely. Don't want any hustle in the music.❞ JUNE, 1976

❝It's a Rastaman playing so it must be a Rastaman Vibration!
And we're serious about the vibration we're putting into ALL our
records, not just this one.❞ JUNE, 1976

❝Rastaman Vibrations gonna cover the earth! Like the water cover
the sea!❞ JUNE, 1976

❝It's not music right now, we're dealing with a message. Right
now the music not important, we're dealing with a message.
'Rastaman Vibration' is more like a dub kinda album and it's come
without tampering y'know. Like 'War' or 'Rat Race', the music
don't take you away, it's more to listen to.❞ JUNE, 1976

'Kaya'

❝'Kaya' means herb. It's a password some of the brethren use in JA.
So 'Kaya' is really dealing with togetherness and humanity and
peace, (because) the thing of peace travel through the earth now.
Yes, 'Rastaman Vibrations' and 'Exodus' were 'arder. This time we
dealing with something softer.❞ FEBRUARY, 1978

❝You have to be you and make the crowd follow you. Like when
we was doin' 'Kaya' we knew that plenty people was gonna say
"Kaya, bla blah blah". But we still do it y'know. Everyone must
take the pressure sometime.❞ SEPTEMBER, 1980

❝Maybe if I'd tried to make a heavier tune than 'Kaya' they
would have tried to assassinate me because I would have
come too hard. I have to know how to run my life,
because that's what I have and nobody can tell me to
put it on the line, you dig? People that aren't involved

don't know it, it's my work and I know it outside in. I know when everything is cool, and I know when I tremble, you understand?**"**

SEPTEMBER, 1979

Many people at first identified with the raw anger in The Wailers' music. Some now claim that you've become rather mellow.

"No man! It might mellow to the outside people but where I come from it is more militant than it ever used to be. Our music is there to deal with the conditions where we come from." SEPTEMBER, 1980

'Punky Reggae Party'

"In a way, me like see them safety pins and t'ing. Me no like do it myself y'understand, but me like see a man can suffer pain without crying.**"** JULY, 1977

'Redemption Song'

"It feel nice. (It was the first one we've done like that) for a long while. We used to do things like that one time, things I call lyrical spirikle, just guitar, drums and singing, some kind of folk song spiritual. 'Redemption Song' strong. It's a real situation natural to I and I.**"** AUGUST, 1980

RECORDS & SONGS

❝It have meaning, you know. I would love to do more like that. What was the lyric in 'Redemption Song' about atomic energy? 'Have no fear for atomic energy/cause none a them can stop the time'. Time is where we are, what we have y'know. And no-one can stop the time. So I say 'have no fear for atomic energy' to those who would put the fear into mankind that everything must be destroyed. Now dem seh this atomic thing can do it, but me seh 'have no fear' because man have hopes. No one can stop the time and you have to live within time. So time is important.❞ SEPTEMBER, 1980

'Burnin' And Lootin'

❝Dat song about burnin' and a-lootin' illusions. The illusions of the capitalists and dem people with the big bank accounts.❞

MARCH, 1976

'Trenchtown Rock'

❝Me write a song called 'Trenchtown Rock'. 'One good t'ing about music, when it hits you feel no pain'. You can talk of the experience in music so after a while it becomes good that you went through all this experience. Music can express it like nothing else can.❞ AUGUST, 1980

'Them Belly Full'

❝Your belly's full, but we're hungry for the love of our brethren. Food might be in your belly, but there's more to living than just filling it. Where's the love of your brother?❞ MARCH, 1976

'I Shot The Sheriff'

❝I want to say 'I shot the police' but the government would have made a fuss so I said 'I shot the sheriff' instead... but it's the same idea: justice.❞ APRIL, 1974

❝**Someone did tell me Clapton was doing the record and it sound great, and it did happen he do it right. We try our own (version) but it couldn't be a hit single because the quality wasn't there at the time. But when someone do over a song them can hear what you did and try and improve on what you do. Maybe they can make it a bit better than the first person who do it.**❞ 1974

❝That message a kind of diplomatic statement. You have to kinda suss things out. 'I Shot The Sheriff' is like I shot wickedness. That's not really a sheriff, it's the elements of wickedness. The elements of that song is people been judging you and you can't stand it no more and you explode, you just explode.❞

JULY, 1975

RECORDS & **SONGS**

"Clapton asked me about the song because when Clapton finished the song he didn't know the meaning of the song. Him like the kind of music and him like the melody and then him make 'I Shot The Sheriff'. I don't know if (he did it) because Elton John say 'Don't Shoot Me, I'm Only The Piano Player', Bob Dylan say 'Take the badge off me, I can't shoot them anymore' and this one man say 'I Shot The Sheriff'. That song never fit no one else but Eric Clapton, right beside Elton John and Bob Dylan." JULY, 1975

'Get Up, Stand Up'

"That song say man can live." 1975

"How long must I protest the same thing? I sing 'Get Up Stand Up' and up 'til now people don't get up. So must I still sing 'Get Up, Stand Up'? I am not going to sing the same song again... I do not want to be a prisoner. I don't want to see people suffer and sing as if I'm glad to see people suffer and to make money off of that. I want people to live big and have enough." APRIL, 1978

'Smile Jamaica'

"I said 'Smile you're in Jamaica'. I didn't say 'Smile Jamaicans, be a Jamaican'. I don't deal with that, a whole bag o'fuckery that."

APRIL, 1977

'Uprising'

❝The (1980 Jamaican) hurricane? I feel it was good and we were lucky for sure, but the hurricane was to show the Jamaicans that God is God and yet them still go on like them don't believe. That's why in 'We And Them Uprising' I wrote 'It seems like total destruction is the only solution.' Which means that it seems like total destruction is still what these people want.❞ SEPTEMBER, 1980

'Bad Card'

❝Someone call from Jamaica and tell me one political party is using 'Bad Card'. Music is music. It heal the scars.❞

'Could You Be Loved'

Did the song have a disco influence?

❝Yes. I just write a song called 'Slogans' (AKA 'Can't Take Your Slogans No More') which is roots. Strictly root. Hear the word. You see, people appreciate a variety of things. Like some man

when he was a child he wish he had a tie. He think when he grow big him can afford ties, him get all sort of ties! It's like the music: naturally if I go to America and hear that type of music, the music is in the air there. If I pick up the guitar now I have a choice. You can try something that music (try to play the music you heard) and that music have root too. You can try something or you can try the other thing and go deeper.❞ AUGUST, 1980

RECORDS & SONGS ❞

BOB MARLEY *Talking*

'Exodus'

Does it sound different because it was recorded in England?

"No. We're all on it, seven of us, right? And it's roots music so if one man get too giddy, the other all seh 'Hey, him gettin' giddy!' I mean, him (guitarist Junior Marvin) get too psychedelic and the islands don't like that, not a giddy man." MAY, 1977

"I wouldn't say I get fed up. If things nah go right then you don't really get fed up, you keep on doing it. I don't get fed up, I love the music." AUGUST, 1980

"Marley's music is always Marley's music. I haven't changed my musical sound. A man plays his music according to the way he feels." DECEMBER, 1979

"Positive vibrations man. That's what makes it work. That's reggae music. You can't look away because it's real. You listen to what I sing because I mean what I sing, there's no secret, no big deal. Just honesty, that's all." 1977

Reggae

Is the aim of your music to convert whites to listen, or is it basically a music by Blacks for Blacks?

"Reggae can't do anything on its own. God say: until the philosophy which places one race superior and another inferior is permanently discredited and abandoned, then we won't have no peace."

JUNE, 1976

"If you play music, or listen to music and you don't know why you playing or listening except for money and pleasures, you can be in serious trouble. Reggae say something. But it can only mean something if it mean something to the people who make it and the people who listen." JUNE, 1976

What's the actual relationship between you and the other Jamaican musicians such as Toots and Jimmy Cliff? Is there a common feeling that you're all together in a movement?

"I don't know. We meet occasionally but we don't visit. Y'see, everybody's working hard, busy. Have to be creating all the while. But we are good brethren." JUNE, 1976

"I met Taj Mahal the other day and he said 'This music you're playing man, it's played in Ethiopia'. So you can see what kind of music this is, this is reggae, the King's music." SEPTEMBER, 1974

"Big Youth? Well, me personally dig Big Youth, like him, the things he do. And Toots (& the Maytals) and The Heptones. The majority of the brothers that try. Some of the brothers try, some don't. I hear plenty bad reggae. Some of the people doing reggae, them's not really where the music is. Them don't really improve, they play something they hear. That becomes stagnant reggae." JUNE, 1976

BOB MARLEY *Talking*

"You've got to appreciate (recognise) the foolish ones, the guys play reggae skanap, skanap skanap. Not my type of reggae that. My reggae unncha, cha unncha cha... more rootsie!" JUNE, 1976

"I don't see reggae music as like 'The Twist', I see reggae music as music. When people say 'reggae' they expect a type of music. As far as me is concerned I never give it a name. I just play music. Once you put it in a bag and call it reggae and then maybe you listen and think you hear a single thing. Because music wide, music go everywhere." JULY, 1975

"This music man, is not music of a day. It have to be real."

JULY, 1975

"The music (reggae) is like the news. The music influence the people, the music do everything fe (for) the people. The music tell the people what to do in Jamaica." SEPTEMBER, 1980

"I don't care what people do with the music. Every time I play, I get fresh inspiration. It fresh, and no-one can hear a song that you write until it out on a record. So people can capitalise on reggae as much as they want. We can play different music from the kind of music we play now. So if someone try to catch up with we, we can leave and change again because that's what we've been doing over the years. Every time we make some music and they catch up with we so we change, just like ska, rocksteady, reggae. If them come too much and call it reggae, we go to nyahbingi music, the first music. It mean 'death to black and white oppressors'. That type of music come from the heart. Every time you hear the drums you hear it, sometime soft, sometime frightening, you get to know it. Like when I first hear rasta drumming, I think something terrible going to do to me because it's something we no understand. And yet it's so near to me. And then we get to understand it and everything become natural again." JULY, 1975

BOB MARLEY *Talking*

"Of course, I'm not a great singer. There's a whole heap of singers coming out of Jamaica that are better than I." AUGUST, 1980

Your favourite group at present is Burning Spear? Do you feel they've copied you?

"Well, I wouldn't say he copied me, but it does sound like he's done some listening!" AUGUST 1975

"Reggae is a music that has plenty fight. But only the music should fight, not the people." 1977

"Reggae doesn't have to be political, or angry. It can be about anything. Most things are worth making music about." 1977

Does reggae originate with Rastafarians?

"Yeah! That's where reggae comes from." JUNE, 1975

"Reggae kinda come from a Spanish, Latin word, and it mean 'King Music'." MAY, 1977

"You getting a three in one music. You getting a happy rhythm with a sad sound with a good vibration... it's roots music." JUNE, 1975

"(Reggae) is what you call international music, complete music. Any music you want play inside of reggae, you can put it here. But it's the rhythm now, that is reggae. Proud rhythm, man, that rhythm can't end. It have a different touch. It's earth rhythm, roots! So you find it can't go out (stop), it's like from the beginning of time, (from) creation." JUNE, 1975

"Blessed reggae is a reggae when you deal with reality. You get more music, more anything. You feel dirt, the earth. You feel it, different from just thinking about it." JUNE, 1975

"Reggae music is a raasclaat music where you have to be proud, you have to know what creation is. So you have a feeling now, so you come out, reach for a chalice. You don't wanna hear no rock music because you can't do that right now. 'Cause rock music calls for neon lights, plenty lights. See, (with) a good reggae music now, you can be anywhere. You can be in the hills."

JUNE, 1975

REGGAE

"No dance look pretty as reggae dance! You can dance the whole night and it keep you in a mood. You love yourself when you dance reggae music. You proud of yourself, you come like you born again. A feeling come in the music like you baptised. Music is great. Music can carry you to some places where you don't know. Carry you to Zion." JUNE, 1975

"Reggae musicians have been accused of selling Jamaican culture. It is not selling our culture. If God hadn't given me a song to sing I wouldn't have a song to sing. Ya kyaan (can't) sell culture."

JUNE, 1976

"Why don't you hear reggae on Jamaican radio? It's because the music shows the real situation in Jamaica. Some people don't like to hear the real truth. Radio is important, but once song come out and you don't hear it on radio, the big promotion is that the song is banned and when song is banned everyone want fe hear it."

JUNE, 1976

"Reggae going to get a real fight, it happen already. This is Third World music. Ya don't have understanding in one day, ya have it little by little and it just grow." MARCH, 1976

"You can't be in a rush to play reggae, lookin' to make a million for it. You can make a million if you want, like Johnny Nash, but the creative purpose suffers. You've got to ask yourself: 'If I can play other kinds of music, why am I playing this kind?' I play it because I love the feel, the expressiveness— not the money." 1975

Music

"If God had'na given me a song to sing, I wouldn't have a song to sing. The song comes from God, all the time." JUNE, 1976

"Reggae music, soul music, rock music —every song is a sign." JUNE, 1976

"Soul, jazz, reggae, calypso, blues—I like plenty good music. Jazz, that's a complete music. Music with feeling. I don't like music or anything that deal with the wrong things of life because I only want to deal with the truth."

JUNE, 1976

"How I learn to play guitar? I teach myself. A good guitar player, him can do some real showy things, but when him a catch you watching, him a-hide it. Like a man a-hide his high cards. He don't want you to catch it so quick." FEBRUARY, 1976

"America: is pure devilry the things that go on there. Them just work with force and brutality. Them lock out the punk thing because they see something is happening... so the oppressors bring another man to blind the youth to the truth, and they call him—John Tra-vol-ta!" MARCH, 1979

BOB MARLEY *Talking*

"Me listen to almost everyone but me no remember names. Me love Stevie Wonder, Curtis Mayfield, Marvin Gaye..."

MARCH, 1978

"I'm a self-taught guitar player. Me like guitarists like Ernest Ranglin." JUNE, 1975

"I used to hear about Bob Dylan plenty. You can say something now; growing up in the ghetto, you don't really get no money for going out and buying recordings. You know what I mean? In time you have money to buy food to eat. So me hear about Dylan's music over the radio. I might go to somebody's house, and they have Bob Dylan and play it. But me never seriously listen to Bob Dylan, until the other day me start, like listening. Because me have people around me who directly, them love music so them become like music freaks. Them invite me out and say, 'Come! want you to listen to some music'. We both have the best herb, the best food, and so we listen to some music 'cause this mon have, like, Richie Havens and them guys there."

"Bob Dylan? Him really say it clear." JANUARY, 1976

"Anything can happen in music, we only experiment. It's never wise to limit yourself. Them people think that I should do the same this year as last! Maybe them people don't like it, but new people like it. You can't stay in one place." APRIL, 1974

What do you think about 'Master Blaster', Steele Wonder's tribute to you?

"I think it's great, I love it. Stevie is the greatest. Stevie didn't tell me he was going to do it but someone who was in the studio with him called me and told me about it."

Aren't you the Master Blaster?

"Yeah, Mastah Blastah... it's nice, y'know." SEPTEMBER,1980

Are you into punk?

❝Listen, punk love reggae and some a dem seh things that Babylon no like. I thought dem was badness first, but now me give dem nine hundred per cent right. Dem resist the society and seh 'Me a punk cos I don't want you to shove me where I don't like it'. Because him nuh feel like we inferior—white man feel inferior to the black man, that's why him try kill the black man. And the punk say: 'No! We wanna join wit' the Rastaman and get something outta life'.❞ JULY, 1977

Does white reggae sound right to you?

❝I hear 'Police And Thieves', you know, dem Clash. And I hear some more y'know. Some I like, some... ah... depends on the feeling. Reggae music is a feeling but reggae music is not the first time that feeling come onto the earth. That feeling is always there with the people, black and white. Even with ordinary people who nuh deal with making no music. If dem hum something, it reggae dem hum without even knowing. It's the same feeling like all the blues and folk come from.❞ SEPTEMBER, 1980

❝I hear The Police do something one time and I figure it kinda nice. It's not Jamaica it's coming from but it still sound good.❞

SEPTEMBER, 1980

WITH RITA MARLEY (LEFT) AND JULY MOWATT

" Me sing one of The Beatles song. Cover one of The Beatles songs—'And I Love Her'. 'I give ya all my love, that's all I dooo'. The thing was we meet and shake hand and say great— them dude they nice. I really like meet them and sit down and chat with them. They're are bredrens. Jah just love roots. Those guys are roots. Them guys are all right, ya know. There is like a king and a queen, ya know—those guys are *roots*. **"** 1975

" The thing that mek the music nice is the music never perfect. So how can I approach it so that I can get the best out of it? But something must go wrong somewhere so I say have a go again. It become interesting for me to work the music then move on, find some new feelings. **"** AUGUST, 1980

" Understand, see musicians get mad because of music. Living my place in Jamaica a man might have a guitar and it drop on brick and the man get mad because he never get another guitar again for a long while. A musician he must search to find a certain phrase and him just can't find it, it trip him out in the head, y'know. Music is a delicate thing in the sense that it tek so much inspiration, you have to be there at all times. Same thing happen to me. **"** AUGUST, 1980

" Some music can't go in a class or a bracket. Music free and without prejudice. Music don't care... music just wanta be. All you have to do is make sure them things in tune. 'Cause when it don't tune, music vex. And when music vex, it don't sound good. That means guitar not tuned, they all gone flat! It's weird, it's foolish, not pleasing to the ear. But if the tune rung! rung! rung! you know, then it must be nice. But if something wrong, every ear hears it. **"**
JUNE, 1975

" You can't rate music with popularity. You have a guy who can play so much good music and him don't even go in the studio. **"**
JUNE, 1975

MUSIC

Politics

"Here comes a man like me saying 'Don't vote!' Rasta no vote."
SEPTEMBER, 1980

Have you ever been involved with politics or politicians?

"Boy, them will use all sort of influence fe try... but the thing is me no like the type of politics that go on. Them want take 'way the job from the people who never vote fe them." SEPTEMBER, 1975

Is it too personal to ask who you might support in the (1980 Jamaican) election?

"Well, I would not support anyone. I'll support myself, a Rasta, you know what I mean? Only Rasta. No one else is what the people want. Everything's our territory." **SEPTEMBER, 1980**

"All we see happening in politics in Jamaica is that a lot of youths — youths that can't even vote – die. Politicians don't care: I mean, maybe you're sick, maybe you want see a doctor, but him don't care about that, him want you to vote. So me no defend politics." SEPTEMBER, 1980

"Politics no interest me. Dem Devil business. They say they will straighten out Jamaica in three months. The purse, you know, won't go around the table, yet they must (claim they can) straighten out Jamaica in three months and everybody lie. Dem a play with people's minds. Never play with people's minds."
FEBRUARY, 1976

BOB MARLEY *Talking*

"To tell you the truth I don't like talking about Jamaica. I can say good things about the people, but the people who run it... I don't wanna say anything because they might charge me with treason when I go back." JULY, 1973

"We tryin' to make things easier but, y'know, the politics keep its teeth. You have two parties fighting each other so we come like nutten (nothing) because them guys always fighting and claiming to be the big guys. Plenty people (in Jamaica) fight for jobs, so the only way to get a job is to be on one side or the other otherwise you suffer, you suffer and they hurt you bad. They burn houses with people in it, babies in it, in Jamaica, you know. I don't really understand it bwoy, really can't understand that. And I know it's the politicians doing it; it's the youth that catches the place afire but it's the politicians' influence. So you can see how nasty it is. You can't burn houses and burn babies: that really not look good. Politics nasty." **JUNE, 1976**

Do the politicians know about you?

"Yeah mon... they no like me 'cos I talk against the system. Some of them say 'Well Bob, you're nice'. They're looking for me like aluminium (Jamaica's main export) y'know, so I can bring some money in. I'm not interested in that, I'm interested in what's happening to the people. I mean, I really like to walk down the street and everyone smile at me instead of suffer. Guys suffer so much they don't have time to smile. The politicians cause it." JUNE, 1976

You've spent nearly the whole year away from Jamaica. Do you miss it?

"No, I don't mind too much. It's a long time to be away from yard (home) but it's the best thing because when ya hear that voting come stay away 'cause it's bad if they wan fe (want to) come close again. But the (1980) hurricane cool off the violence a little bit. Maybe, them say it was a political hurricane."

SEPTEMBER, 1980

"It's worse (in Jamaica) than it ever used to be in the sense of political pressure. A lot of people dying every day. Some of dem I know. People no see where dem things are leading and that dem have an alternative — Rasta. Dem cause so much fight against Rasta because Rasta is the only redemption to fight. But this pressure, it not Rasta fight. We're not fighting a revolution down there. Two people fight, it's madness. Double wrong. People in Jamaica, dem have guns. Where people get the guns? Government give people the guns. Right now it explode mon. Something bad have to happen. One of dem (cause of troubles) American and the other Russian." AUGUST, 1980

"I defend Haile Selassie but right now in Ethiopia they don't like any talk of Selassie. The government there don't like Rasta either because them bring off propaganda and want to change to a kind of Russian tradition. So I man say it's nice to go there but I don't really feel the strength is there. Not until things change with the government and the people become the people again." 1980

"Government sometimes maybe don't like what we have to say because what we have to say too plain." JUNE, 1975

"Only one government me love, the government of Rastafari." JUNE, 1976

What do you think of the Strategic Arms Limitation Treaty?

"Let them perish in their own fucking SALT !" 1978

WITH PRIME MINISTER MICHAEL MANLEY (LEFT) AND
JAMAICAN LABOUR PARTY LEADER EWARD SEAGA AT THE
ONE HOME PEACE CONCERT IN JAMAICA, 1978

POLITICS

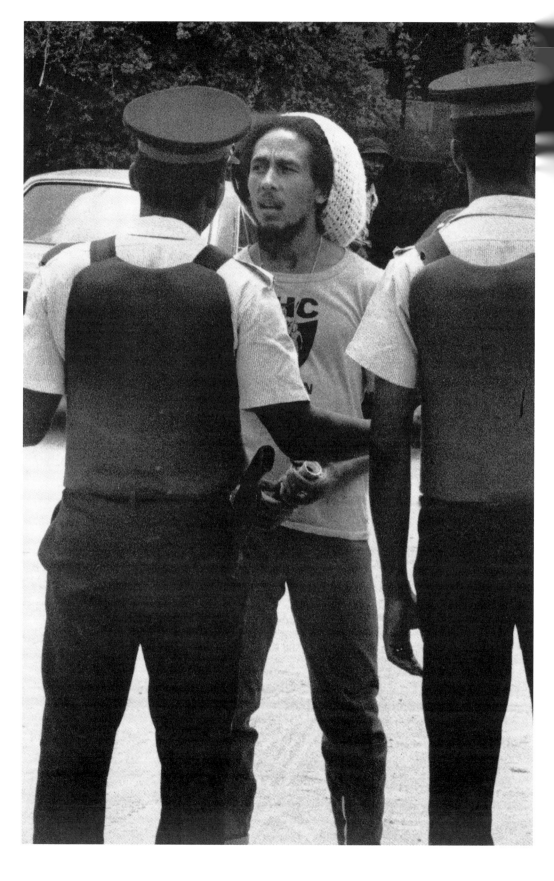

Struggle

"What we (black people) really want is the right to be right and the right to be wrong." **JUNE, 1976**

"My music fights against the system that teaches to live and die." JUNE, 1976

"Is them guys ya (pointing to establishment figures in a comic strip) who the black man figure will give them the power. You can't let them be the leader for you. Them guys take the new wine, them not going to change. We make them be our problem. But them don't exist if you don't want them fe exist. You fe (have to) deal with the youth." **SEPTEMBER, 1975**

"Trenchtown is a town anywhere you come from. If you come from Trenchtown, you don't stand a chance. Dat's a fact." FEBRUARY, 1976

"You know why I don't love Jamaica society? Because dem fightin' is madness. Dem things make blood run feared." **FEBRUARY, 1976**

"I go to jail one time for no driver licence!" FEBRUARY, 1976

"Me go down to jail one time in Jamaica, and me go to jail one time in England. When I was put in jail in Jamaica, I drive a car and somebody in the car was like a... no, a guy was driving the car without a licence, and when the police happen he tell them I was teaching him to drive. So them teach me for abidding and abetting. Circumstances in England is that one time some guys who was smoke herb, and them claim some herb was coming into England, and them come check out our place one time and find one of the guys who's seller was there. Them hold him and tell us we were responsible for the house. And them hold me too. But it was

BOB MARLEY *Talking*

nothing. I stay in jail and two, three hours, and them let me go. I stayed in jail in Jamaica for six hours, or less than that. I went to court and they say, 'okay, you can go'. **99** 1975

66 Plenty people have to die. Don't ask me why. Wickedness must be destroyed. 99 FEBRUARY, 1976

66 There's a revolution going on right now, but not one like with an army. It's snipers, snipers, through the night. **99** APRIL, 1974

66 Me always live in... in the ghetto. Me don't feel like the ghetto should be my future like we should always love live (living) in a shit. 99 MARCH, 1978

66 The kids grow up and they see their father go to work and suffer and die and mother got a big belly goes to hospital and takes an operation. Their (family) structure is damaged and they've got to keep it together. The children have got to keep it together... cos they're youth them really know (about suffering). **99** JUNE, 1976

66 Kids who come and see you over here relate to you in a different way. Them relate to me more as street struggling against system pressure. A lot of people relate to the same t'ing but kinda more involved in a sense of belief and the roots. System up against I and I, 'cause before there was system there was I and I and them mek the system fight against I and I. System fight, and we just say peace, love and this is a way of life. It no we against the system, it the system against we. 99 AUGUST, 1980

"So much people have to die to make the other people not even live but see the mistake that those that die make. To think what's going on down there man (Jamaica), it is a dreadful t'ing. It's like some mass execution, without control or anything. And Jamaica is a likkle place. Jamaica is sufferin' people who have nutten else. All dem do is fight. For what? For nothing. Dem not fight for Jah or anything. Just war." **AUGUST, 1980**

"Anyone who cry out fe justice is a Wailer." 1974

"Like Jah say, the West must perish. It's Devil's country all right. Devils are real people and capitalism and penalism (are a) type of devilism and Draculazing. It's Devil controlling, Devil running part of the earth while God is in Africa waiting for we to agree that there's Devil running this. **JUNE, 1975**

STRUGGLE

BOB MARLEY *Talking*

"You have to be a sufferer to say to yourself, 'Feeling alright'."

APRIL, 1976

"Here (Jamaica) y'kyaan work fe what ya want. Ya can never reach the goal. The system kill people so we must kill the system. Every mon want fe drive car, nobody wants to ride donkey." JUNE, **1976**

"I don't like guns and I don't want to fight. But when we move to go to Africa, if they say no, then I personally will have to fight. I don't love fightin' but I don't love wickedness either. My father was a captain in the army; I guess I have a kinda war thing in me, but it is better to die fightin' for our freedom than to be a prisoner all the days of your life." AUGUST, 1978

"Ahh, Jamaica. Where can your people go? I wonder if it's anyplace on this earth." **1975**

"You have to be someone." JULY, 1979

"When I lived in the ghetto, every day I had to jump fences, police trying to hold me, you dig? So my job all the while was to try to find one place where the police wouldn't run me down too much. So I don't want to stay in contact with the ghetto. In contact with the ghetto means in contact with a prison, not the people. When the law (police) comes out, they send them into the ghetto first, not uptown. So how long does it take you to realise— bwoy, well they don't send them uptown, so we'll make a ghetto uptown. You either stay there (downtown) and let bad people shoot you down or you make a move and show people some improvement. Or else I would take up a gun and start shoot them off and then a lot of youths would follow me and they'd be dead the same way. I want some improvement. It doesn't have to be materially, but it can be freedom of thinking." **1979**

❝I expect if you're living by the gun, if the gun is the fight, then FIRE gun. If where you're coming from you fight with sticks and stones, then fight with sticks and stones. If the fight is spiritual, then fight spiritual, because everywhere the fight goes on. We don't have any alternatives.❞ 1979

❝People say we're involved in some big war and fight—it won't be like that. You see, they're not fighting against sin. I wouldn't fight a war, I'd use righteousness, try to live and go home. The revolution is a mechanical thing you know—they've planned it. If you plan revolution, you can get hurt. Revolution is not planned. It just happens and you can see it going on around you. The only control you have is if Jah really loves you and he takes you from the revolution. The revolution'll go on, herder, but pure fighting. Not like the Cuban revolution —the whole universe is involved in this revolution.❞ **1975**

❝Me no really want to talk about revolution until me have guns, right? So me no want talk about revolution 'cos me nuh know if me ever get guns. Y'see, we don't make guns y'know. I want check ya now (understand me): even in Africa, we find seh the gun me kill my brother with, is white man we 'ave fe buy the gun from.❞ JUNE, 1978

❝Music is the biggest gun, because it save. It nuh kill, right? The other gun lick off ya head!❞

JUNE, **1978**

STRUGGLE ❞❞

His Message

"God never made no difference between black, white, blue, pink or green. People is people, y'know. That is the message we try to spread." JUNE,1976

"I have a duty to tell the truth as I have been told it. I will keep on doing it until I am satisfied the people have the message that Rastafari is the almighty and all we black people have redemption just like anyone else. Not for money will I do anything man, but because I have something to do."

JUNE, 1976

"They're different songs, written so that more people can understand the words. I always write about situations and my thoughts on life." JULY, 1973

"I don't see how you can leave your roots. As long as you write a song and play it, it must be roots." APRIL 1974

BOB MARLEY *Talking*

66It's no great pleasure to sing about suffering because me no feel like people should really suffer and it is not a great thing to sing about suffering. But you have to sing about it because it a go on.99

FEBRUARY, 1978

66**What I'm saying is what I'm saying, y'know: the audience supposed to know what I'm saying before they come. Sometimes maybe they don't understand, sometimes they get really high.**99 JUNE, 1976

66It's a universal, international message. 'Cause you get up and you quarrel every day, you really just saying prayers to the Devil because the Devil like you when you quarrel and war every day.99

JUNE, 1976

66**It easy to write an ordinary love song, y'know: 'Hey baby I love you but you don't treat me good'. But that don't really interest me any more, it don't live long. If you sing the right words it can live. It can live through this world and when the next world comes you don't need that anymore, there you need new words.**99 JUNE, 1976

66Sometimes I can dig instrumental music. But lyrics important. The whole thing complete is the important thing. People who listen to the music and don't listen to the words soon start listening to the words. As long as you want to listen, you hear the words even if you don't understand everything.99 **JULY, 1975**

66**Overcome the devils with a thing named love.**99 JUNE, 1975

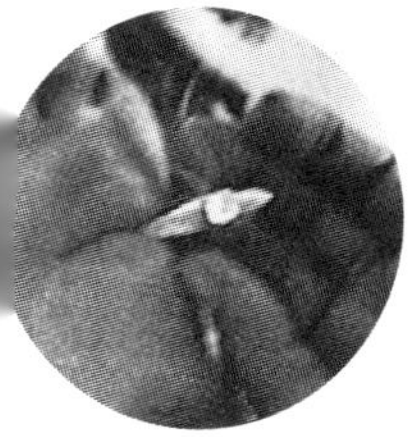

“Ya have fe be careful of the type of song and vibration that ya give fe the people, for ‘woe be unto they who lead my people astray’. As a singer I personally like to sing for the people rather than sing for half the people.” **JUNE, 1976**

“The message is to live. My message across the world is Rastafari. Right now, no-one teachin’ the real way of life.” MARCH, 1976

“These songs, people understand them or they cyaan (can’t) understand them, but y’ave fe sing them just the same. What people want is the beauties, man.” **AUGUST, 1976**

“I’m a man of God and me come to do God’s work.” JUNE, 1975

Rasta

"Rastafari not a culture, it's a reality." **FEBRUARY, 1976**

"Me can't tell you how me know Ras Tafari. It is pure vision."
FEBRUARY, 1976

How do you relate to Haile Selassie's death last August (1975)?

"Death? Don't speak of death. I don't look upon His Majesty as a man. Jah dead. Jah can't dead! His Imperial Majesty got spirit." **FEBRUARY, 1976**

"My future is righteousness." FEBRUARY, 1976

"During my time when I was a young lickle Rasta youth me just try to enjoy myself in Rasta work. When me see anything red, gold and green me check it serious, like it's coming as a message. When me look 'pon the street life me see that red, gold and green control the earth: anywhere you go on earth the stop light is red, gold and green. It's scientific and psychological." **NOVEMBER, 1979**

When did you become a Rasta?

"Well, I ever was, ever is, and ever will be, Rasta."

How long have you been a Rasta?

"From creation." 1973

"The greatest thing them (the church) can say is about death — them say you die and go to heaven after all this sufferation. To go through all this sufferation for that! It's like after me sick me go to the doctor. No, the greatest thing is life." JULY, 1975

BOB MARLEY *Talking*

BOB MARLEY *Talking*

"Babylon no wan' peace, man. Babylon want power."

APRIL, 1977

"You change if you change from Babylon to Rasta, but you can't change from Rasta to anything. When the truth awaken in you you can't do anything but accept the truth." MARCH, 1978

"God is not partial man. Selassie I blow breath into a man so why the people watch the bank account? Why they no watch the heart that beat?" **JUNE, 1976**

"I pledged to work for righteousness. God's given me inspiration. God is the boss, he tell you what to do." JUNE, 1976

"Man can't do without God. Just like you're thirsty, you have to drink water. You just can't do without God." **JUNE, 1976**

"You must understand, God is everliving and Haile Selassie is God, God is not everybody. Some people say 'I'm a man, you're a man' and they look upon a man and say 'That man God'. It's not like that, a man have to prove himself to be God: Haile Selassie is God." JUNE, 1976

"Watch now how a hurricane comes (1980), heading straight for Jamaica. At the last minute, Jah turn it. You can imagine what could have happened down there? The hurricane was to show Jamaicans that God is God and yet them still go on like them don't believe."

SEPTEMBER, 1980

"Babylon is everywhere. You have wrong and you have right. Wrong is what we call Babylon. I could have been born in England, I could have been born in America. It make no difference where me born because there is Babylon everywhere."

In Addis Ababa too?

"Yeah. What is important is man should live in righteousness, in natural love for mankind. I was born in Babylon. My father who got together with my mother was a English guy who was a captain of the army, who go to war. You can't get more Babylon than that. My mother was a black woman from the inner centre of Jamaica, real country, and this was a man who come from England and go war. So look how far Babylon come from England." JULY, 1975

"A certain word can hold you out from the truth a long while; like people can use the word Babylon and have no understanding of what Babylon is. So he becomes an idiot, he becomes more chained 'cause a thing is right or wrong. If you're right you're right, if you're wrong you're wrong." JULY, 1975

"I am one of the Twelve Tribes Of Israel and we are trying to unite the people so that we can move back to Africa. The Twelve Tribes are the twelve sons of Israel, representing the twelve tendencies of man from Reuben to Benjamin so that every man is born in one of the 12 months and each month is represented by a tribe. So like for me, come from the Tribe Of Joseph, and Haile Selassie the conquering lion is of the Tribe Of Judah." FEBRUARY, 1978

RASTA

BOB MARLEY *Talking*

How come you're aware of the danger of being assassinated when you say there is no such thing as death?

"Hold on, now. You think you can go out there and lay down in front of a car and let it run over you? If I go outside and see the big bus coming and put my head underneath it, what do you think will happen? I don't believe in death, neither in flesh nor in spirit. But you have to avoid it. Some people don't figure it's such a great thing. They don't know how long they can preserve it. Preservation is the gift of God, the gift of God is life, the wages of sin is death. When a man does wickedness he's gone up there and dead." JULY, 1979

"When you're dead, you're dead." JUNE, **1978**

"**The only truth is Rastafari.**" AUGUST, 1980

"HIM (Haile Selassie I) ever young, the youngest man on earth, him control time." **JULY, 1975**

"Rastafari is like... the turtle, with a shell all over him. You got to have Rasta protection. That mean if a man is trying to hurt you, in five minutes time he might drop asleep and in six minutes time you go out there and him gone. You go out on street with herb and meet police(man) and him a search. Another guy go out on the street and say 'Alright, think about it first'. You feel go out on street now. You go out and street cool. The police round corner dere. Certain time, man just go out there and him get search right away and him say 'Bloodclaat, how did this happen?' It just time control and if him move a little bit earlier or a later him gonna miss it. That's why Rasta is the only shield. It a time when brothers fight against brothers, sisters against sisters, mankind against mankind. All dem thing is a sign of the time. The only survival is Rasta. AUGUST, 1980

"I don't believe, you know. When you believe, you have doubts. You have to know. I know that His Imperial Majesty Haile Selassie is God Almighty. That's what I know." **1975**

How does your religion affect your music?

"Religion can't really affect the music. Music is natural, y'know. Me don't have a religion... me natural, not a religion, just a natural thing you suppose to have." JUNE, 1975

RASTA

What does Rasta mean?

"Righteousness." JUNE, 1975

Would Rasta settle for making Jamaica like Africa?

"No! No settle for Jamaica. We like Jamaica, y'know. But Jamaica is spoiled as far as Rastaman is concerned. The history of Jamaica is spoiled, just like if ya have an egg that break ya kyaan (can't) put it back together again. Jamaica can't be fixed for I and I, for Rastaman. When we check out the system here, we see death, and Rastaman say life!" JUNE, 1976

"Every man fe himself, and God for us all. Yeh man! This is war! Jamaica is hell y'know. Until we can find our roots again, politics will still be a thing." JUNE, 1976

"People used to call you 'natty head' as an insult but I use it as a crown, because I think of myself positively. I crown myself with it. You call me natty head—great! Who cares what you think?" 1974

"There are two things in this earth, the good and the bad. Look out into the street you see plenty bad. There is only one Rasta. You say 'You must keep yourself smart and groomed'. I don't know who I must look presentable to, but I know I have to look presentable to myself. Because if I don't like the way I am, I don't see how somebody else wants me to be. My locks are total freedom. They show the people in Babylon that this man is totally free. I'm not under any influence from them anymore. They can't say 'Well boy, you have to do this'. But understand, that's my reason. Some Rasta men grow locks for different reasons." 1974

"**Football is a part of I, keep you out of trouble. Discipline. When you run you clear out your head.**"

"Music is the biggest gun, because it save. It nuh kill, right? The other gun lick off ya head!"

"God created the earth for us, but people wonder, 'Who owns the tree? Who owns the ganja pipe?'"

"I have a BMW. But only because BMW stands for Bob Marley & The Wailers."

❝I want to be a Rastaman and I'd prefer them to kill me instead of telling me what they want me to be. That's how Rastas get such a hard time in Jamaica —nobody gives them any work.❞ 1974

What do you think of people that doubt Rastafari because Selassie died?

❝It's because the people don't realise I say he's God. And if I say he's God, how can someone tell me that God is dead? I know the mysteries and the mystic our God can do. And God doesn't hide himself from man. God's a man who can disappear and appear.❞

1976

❝You know, you're going to have war, big wars, but I'm preparing to meet Jah while other people prepare for war.❞ 1975

❝Anywhere devilism is, is Babylon. Babylon fill the air with bad vibes. The Devil ain't got no power over me. The Devil come and me shake hands with the Devil! Devil has his part to play, Devil's a good friend too, because when you don't know him, that's the time he can mash you down. The Devil's a dangerous guy. Is-a Jah going to protect me. He said fear not, have no fear.❞

Do you fear anything? Me?

❝Nah. Well, me don't swim too tough so me don't go in the water too deep.❞

JULY, 1975

RASTA

Race

Would you not get along very well with non-Rasta people?

"Give a man a chance, you know? I don't want to crucify a man like they crucified Christ, just because he wasn't a Rastaman."

JUNE, 1976

"My music defends righteousness. If you're black and you're wrong, you're wrong; if you're white and you're wrong, you're wrong: if you're indian and you're wrong, you're wrong. It's universal." JUNE, 1976

"There should be no WAR between black and white ! But until white people listen to black with open ears, there must be – well suspicion!" **JUNE, 1976**

"The colour of a man's skin is no more important than the colour of his eyes. I don't try to get a black audience." JUNE, 1978

"I believe in freedom for everyone, not just the black man."

AUGUST, 1989

"Me no talk fe no white and me no talk fe no black. Me just talk fe the Creator and fe that vibration that we must all come together and live." JUNE, 1976

"Can't tell anybody how to live, so everyone have to find out how them wanna live. For God create the earth and everyone as an equal being, so any life them wanna live them have to live it."

APRIL, 1977

BOB MARLEY *Talking*

"Well, me don't dip on nobody's side, me don't dip on the black man's side not the white man's side, me dip on God's side, the man who create me, who cause me to come from black and white, who give me this talent." JULY, 1975

"My father was a white guy, my mother was a black woman, and I came in between. Like, you know, I'm nothing. All I have is God."

1977

"Unity is the world's key, and racial harmony. Until the white man stops calling himself white and the black man stops calling himself black, we will not see it. All the people on earth are just one family." FEBRUARY, 1978

Is it your intention to free the niggers?

"Niggers? Niggers? Nigger mean doom. I a Rasta. You can't free death. I life. Where you get that word nigger from?"

PRESS CONFERENCE. JULY, 1975

"My songs have a message of righteousness whether you're black... listen man, you know I'm not prejudice about myself. Because my father's white, my mother's black. You know what them call me, half-caste or whatever." JULY, 1975

"Noah had three sons, Ham, who was black and lived in Africa, Jaffet who was white and lived in Europe, and Shem, of Asia. White man must be Jaffet, black must be Ham. If a man comes to you and say 'I am blackman' that means war. It means something if a white man come to you and says 'I am Jaffet'. You know he is your bredda (brother)." FEBRUARY, 1978

"The God who mek I and I, him create technicolor people."

AUGUST, 1980

"You can't come tell me about white and black or pink and blue. We fly a colour which is red, gold and green. We're not prejudiced, we leave our judgement to Jah." JUNE, 1975

"Black people are so stubborn.
They stay here because white
people give them a big hotel and
a floor to vacuum.**"** AUGUST, 1974

"Is God who make everybody, and
him make a way for the black man
that the white man have to follow,
because out of the black man
came the white man, all white
men.**"** JULY, 1978

**"You mustn't bow to the white man.
You must be superior to him.
That means you cannot be
prejudice, because if you are
superior, how can you be
prejudice? Now we are not saying
you have to mingle with them
now. But you cannot walk with
that half-and-half thing. We are
superior people but dem guys
(white people) sort of took our
thing and turned it back 'pon we.
You have to show people who God
is... and deal with it.**"** JULY, 1978

"Prejudice is a chain, it can hold
you. If you prejudice, you can't
move, you keep prejudice for
years. Never get nowhere with
that.**"** JULY, 1974

RACE "

Jah

What influences your writing?

"Jah." 1975

"We have a song called 'Jah Live'. Them on the news say that our God is dead. But, you know, is them don't understand. Them don't understand. We have a name, 'Crazy Baldheads', and we have one named 'Roots'. We're gonna chase those crazy baldheads outta town. That's about the system and the things what happen around here. Like, for instance, we build the cabin, we plant the corn, our people slave for this country. Now, you know what I mean, today they look upon me with a scorn. Yet, them eat up all our corn. So we have to chase those crazy baldheads outta town. Ain't nuthin' else we could do. We can't stand and let them bury us. Enough of that sheet! Because we plant the corn, yuh know. We build the cabin, we plant the corn. And we build the country. Yet you have guys that look for Rastaman and say, 'You know Rasta, deh no good ! ' It's our sweat that walk on every day. Our blood and our sweat."

Will you eventually use your power as a musician, or a missionary, of influence?

"I don't think about power. Funny word. God, he has power and he has not stopped working." JUNE, 1976

"I feel now that with the word getting out through the records and that, the words are getting across to the world. Oh yeah. It's not me saying these things, but God." JUNE, 1976

"You know, me can always do what me want to do. Just in time, everything happen in time. You see, God is my father and him grow me just the way a son suppose to be grown. The perfect father for me." JUNE, 1975

BOB MARLEY *Talking*

" Is only one man me ask to make me be a servant unto HIM. Me no wanna do nothin' unless is HIM tell me to do it. You hear what Jah say: 'Until the philosophy which holds one race superior and another inferior...'. No one else have nothin' more to write right now. Me no see nothin' great like that. People have to know that and them have to know who say it. You don't see that God almighty say that? Watch where him come from—Africa. "

AUGUST, 1976

Have you anything to say on Selassie's death?

" Selassie-I, you can check him so. Cos if him eighty-three today, tomorrow you see him and he twenty-eight. And next morning him a baby, and today him a bird. Yeah man! Jah Live! Ya cyaan (can't) kill God. " AUGUST, 1976

" Jah appear to me in a vision—and every time he look just a bit older than me. 'I'm don't look 90 year old or anything. Like if I'm thirty, then 'im look about thirty-five. Man, it's so sweet, it's me brother, me father, me mother, me creator, everything. " 1975

" (My music) must be a gift. Some people call everything a gift. It's a reality. The work just (comes) so you have to do it. This God do all things, you know what I mean? So me personally as a man is nothin' without the inspiration of Jah. " JUNE, 1975

" I am sure Haile Selassie I is almighty God—with no apologies. "

1976

" Facts an' facts, an' t'tings an t'ings: dem's all a lot of fuckin' bullshit. Hear me ! Dere is no truth but de one truth, an' that is de truth of Jah Rastafari. " 1978.

Africa & Repatriation

“We come from Africa and none of the leaders want fe accept it. They want us fe think we are all Jamaicans. The majority of Jamaican people want fe go home to Africa but the leaders say you must stay and die here.” JUNE, 1976

“Today is not the day but when it happen 144,000 of us go home.” JUNE, 1976

“I get the urge that the time is right when the youth unite in Jamaica. Then the time is right for Africa. If you go to Africa when the youth is not unite in Jamaica then something wrong somewhere. Need to have some kinda proof fe walk with.”
FEBRUARY, 1978

When you went to Africa for the Zimbabwe Independence Celebrations (April 18, 1980) you seemed to come back a changed man.

“You can say that again. But I really get the re-charge from Ethiopia because that song ‘Zimbabwe’ was written in a land called Shashamani (in Ethiopia). So you can say it’s a full recharge that, and when the song came out, it just happen. So can you imagine if it was in Ethiopia where you wrote all your songs, then nearly every song you write could happen then maybe somebody would say ‘Boy, he is a prophet’.”
SEPTEMBER, 1980

BOB MARLEY *Talking*

Was the Zimbabwe concert a very emotional experience for you?

66 Strong, y'know. It was very nice. A good experience for me to take part in a t'ing like that. You feel a kind of solidarity with a lot of people who's there. Them support you more than just having the music and just like you have other people who will never really go through the experience them still become a part of it. People just want peace, justice and the right thing. 99 AUGUST, 1980

Why do you want to go back to Ethiopia?

66 Forward. 99 JULY, 1975

66 Rasta man must go home to Africa. It sound funny to some people sometime... like a mad thing. But it is our real desire fe go home to Africa. Certain things that happen a long time ago must be revealed, and until that happen, I and I still in captivity. 99 JUNE,1976

66 **One reason I don't go to Ethiopia (yet) is why am I going to Ethiopia, to spy? To spy if the land is nice and I want to live there? When I go to Ethiopia it have to be natural, like. It can't be just because me have the money for go. Ethiopia is more than that. When we go to Ethiopia, that'll be something. It can't be just a vacation, you know, foolishness. That'll be real.** 99 JULY, 1975

How do you see the current war between Ethiopia and Somalia?

66 The war, when you check to find why they fight, what cause the trouble, and you find Ethiopia was in famine and y'know that they never come and beg help. Everyone know of famine and yet 'mankind' want them to come beggin' for help. So what happen to The Man? Why doesn't he help? If I was Russia or America I would have tried my best and help them 'cause it's not right that two peoples who is the same fight each other. When they was starvin' nobody would help but when they revolt and turn against His Majesty (Haile Selassie I) they have all the ammunition in the world. It's like two neighbours quarrelling and instead of the big

man come between them and say 'stop', they push them together to fight. Somali shoot with Russian guns, Ethiopia shoots with Russian guns, so who benefit from the war?**"** **FEBRUARY, 1978**

"A lot of people defend South Africa, some secretly, some openly. A lot of white people defend South Africa, and when you keep the black man down in South Africa you keep him down all over the earth. Because Africa is Solomon's Goldmine. So—war! Either I and I lives, or no-one lives." 1979

"A guy will look at me and say, 'Hey, how can you think about Africa, look how many people in Africa are starving'. I say, 'Yes my friend, but what can you do to help Africa?' I hope people can really understand because God is God, it's really a mystic thing. People will say, 'How does God live in Ethiopia and the people around him starve?' God doesn't come to just make the people in Ethiopia happy and the rest starve—that wouldn't be God. It's a lucky thing Ethiopia does suffer, to show us that we have a future.**"** 1976

"Too many people going on like only England and America in the world. But there is a better life in Africa. I feel for Africa. I want to go there and write some music. Instead of going to New York, why can't we go to Ghana? Go to Nigeria, meet some black people. Learn a new' language." AUGUST, 1974

"Why should I stay in Jamaica when I want to smoke a spliff that God made and they stop me with force?**"** JUNE, 1976

America

"I was in America 'cause me mother lived there. The pace faster. Definitely. Things go quicker. Difference with America is that you can get things done. Jamaica is a place where you relax and learn to put off things. Ho boy, in America you got to get it boy, you got to get it. Yah. We have Americans come down here. Is a help we get them, like, 'Don't go so fast, watch this. Please don't go so fast'. In America, things a snap! You hear a young girl say, 'Goddamn it! One telephone run Jamaica! I live in a house with twenty telephones and one telephone run Jamaica!" 1975

BACKSTAGE WITH GEORGE HARRISON L.A, 1975

BOB MARLEY *Talking*

Why doesn't black American youth accept reggae?

"Well, in America it's business. In America ya got a lot of record companies so I figure that when the record companies start to pick up on reggae acts we'll begin to get somewhere. So instead of having me alone going out, you'll have me with someone, someone with someone else and the record industry will be interested in the music. Right now them not interested."

SEPTEMBER, 1980

"You ask me what I think about America. It's dat I find plenty people doin' window-shoppin' right in Manhattan. And you know it's just trick, pure trick, the guy dat make the store window and decorate it to catch your eye."

Don't you shop?

"Well, yes sometimes I go look to see if I can find some jeans. I go somewhere down in the (Greenwich) Village." FEBRUARY, 1976

What do you think of New York?

"During my early days when I first sight (understand) Rastafari, maybe I would never come into a building like this. I wouldn't even go into a concrete building in Jamaica, you understand. But then after a while I start to think 'Well there's work to be done. I must deal with this music that God has given me so as this music can carry me'. So me say OK, earthquake can come but if God send me out HIM (His Imperial Majesty) never shake no earthquake upon me so it's not that fate that me a trouble with." SEPTEMBER, 1980

"One time they show me a plan they had for Kingston—and that's Manhattan, New York, New York! I mean, if you go down to Harbor Street there, and look good, there's some high building, and you say, 'What's really happening here? Who's coming in, and putting a lot of weight upon the earth?' And big sky-scrape— going up." 1975

Business

Do you have a recording contract?

"I have a recording agreement."

What's the difference?

"One is an agreement and one is a contract!" JUNE, 1975

Do you choose your own producer?

"No! No! We do our own music. The guy can't really do our music. The guy don't know it, we know it." JUNE, 1975

ISLAND RECORD BOSS CHRIS BLACKWELL

"Those guys on the machine (producers), all they want to do is hustle quick. You find a guy who puts out 200 songs a year with 60 different labels and 900 different singers. And those guys don't play any music, they only have the equipment and they try to make it so that you don't get any money." 1975

"When the thieves took up with reggae music, man, they have it made! It easy in Jamaica for any guy who have a few dollars to rent a studio, go in, get a recording, ask the engineer to mix it. The hustlers move in as soon as he gone into the street: the record goes into the stores and Jojo (the artist) knows nothing about what happened. Jamaicans go slow, everything is 'soon come', but if there's one thing Jamaicans rush about, it's making a recording."

1980

"Before I knew Island and Chris Blackwell, I had some
albums out in England. Three albums of my music on
Trojan Records that I didn't even know about! It's so weird.
That's why some guys get knots in their heads. When you grow
up as a youth, you see people and meet people and talk to
everybody and everybody show you a smiling face because you is
a youth. But when you grow up come now, it something else that
go on, because the same people that used to laugh is the same
people that now go 'Urrrrr' (grumbling). You know? So, there's
plenty fill up the earth. Everybody get ripped off. Every time.
Three albums! I don't think them have any more stuff They can't
do that, 'cause them play out what them have." OCTOBER, 1975

"We have to try to trick the guy who have pirate mind. Sometimes
you release (a record) in Jamaica but you come to New York and
hear the record selling here. Yet nobody have any permission.
So we have to get a big company (to) release it. Big company catch
a guy pressing it, (they) can destroy it. Otherwise he go on and
press it in him basement and keep it under cover and you still in
Jamaica and never know about it. All you can do is when you come
into town you get your gun and go down there and blast away.
So to stop that you deal with a big record company. Stop you
from committing murder. That is how my record deal (with Island)
come about." JUNE, 1975

"Wasn't because of no connection that we go to England
(for a recording contract). The guys (we used to deal with in
England) was some big pirates. Them guys killer of reggae music,
kill rock steady and kill ska. Them guys for reggae music like
(some) people is for rock, y'know, suck out the artist and
sometime them kill him." JUNE, 1975

"The music business, man, you can't question the how, because you
can't know the guy who own the music. Who (is) the guy? You can't
be caring. You have to do what you have to do. Do your own thing
if you want. Some people get trapped, you know." JUNE, 1975

"The only change in the industry as we know it now is the people who do the music, have the music, protect themselves. Because other people just hustlers. You can't have a guy who own record studios and yet him don't know 'G' (musical note). Yet him want capitalise off music so much. The people who do the music should control the thing. Them guys that run it is not able to control it." JUNE, 1975

"We get a raw deal from people and even sometimes it is the black guy (ripping us off) because him don't really get ahead. One day you start think about the business and see all them big guys sit on them desk, just parked out the parking lot like a car. Pure (entirely) big guys control the record business. You must get rip off. The only way you don't get rip off is when you don't do it (music). Once you start, you get rip off." JUNE, 1975

"You know how plenty music get lost? In mixing." JUNE, 1975

How long have you been working professionals?

"How you mean, professionally? Getting paid for it? Now, we always get rip off, but we still was professional!" JUNE, 1975

BUSINESS

"Yes, people rob me and try fe trick me, but now I have experience. Now I know and I see and I don't get tricked. Used to make recordings and not get royalties. Still happen sometime. All Wailers records made here (Jamaica) but them pirated to England. All them English companies rob man. Everybody that deals with West Indian music—thieves." JUNE, 1976

"They don't want fe trick you, them want fe trick your mind, that's the thing I don't like. You have eyes, you have ears, you can talk, you can smell and yet him want fe trick your mind. Is better somebody ask you for something and get it rather than try to trick me fe take it. I know who God is, so how can you trick me? I'm no fool." 1980

"Jamaica is a place where you easily build up competition in your mind. People here feel like they must fight against me and I must fight against you. Sometimes a guy feels like that because he might never have no schoolin' and I went to school so he must feel he sing some song to wipe me off the marker or I should do the same. Jealousy. Suspicion. Anger. Poverty. Competition. We should just get together and create music but there's too much poverty fuckin' it up." JUNE, 1980

"If we are true brothers money is not a separation for us." **JUNE, 1976**

Violence

"Armed struggle? I don't want to fight, but when I move to go to Africa, if they say so, then me personally will have to fight. Me don't love fighting, but me don't love wickedness either." 1975

Many of your fans were frightened of the attempt on your life in December 1976. Has that situation been resolved?

"Well, me don't feel exactly at ease. Me don't know what to say. That was Rasta work it is, we free, and the youth that tried it free. Everybody free. No big mixing up with no court and nobody. Rasta take care of it in his own way." SEPTEMBER, 1980

"It was a miracle. The whole thing was a miracle. No one sees who, no-one catches who and is a miracle that me get saved. So everyone get the miracle, man." FEBRUARY, 1978

"It kinda like this. Me there and then them come through the door and start gun-shootin', blood claat. That mean I couldn't move, one time I moved to one side and the gun shot flew over here (where he was standing) and then I moved this way and the gun shots go here (the other side of him). The feelin' I had got was to run hard but God just moves me in time.

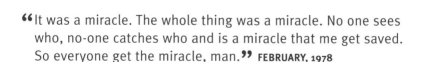

BOB MARLEY *Talking*

His Majesty was directing me and as me moved me felt well high, me just feel like I get high. His Majesty man won't get me shot, But man it's a thing, I tell ya Rasta, dangerous." FEBRUARY, 1978

"It strengthened me, this experience. It hurt me on one arm on one night but me feel the vibes, me know something was going to happen. Me not know exactly what. So when one night I go to bed and in the night my vision say me in a barrage of gun-shot but me can't see who fires the shot, and me like against the wall amid pure gunshot fire but me not get shot, when me wake up me start to think about me vision and realise it very serious vision so me talk with the brethren about it. Here I was and when I first heard gun-shot outside me jump and think to run but remember vision, in vision don't run. I must stay, don't run." **FEBRUARY, 1978**

"I know I was born with a price on my head." MARCH, 1978

Why were you shot?

"Maybe jealousy. Jealousy's a disease inside plenty people brain. It stir 'em up and twist 'em round towards wickedness." **1978**

Do you know who shot you?

"Yeah, but dat top secret. Really top secret." MAY, 1977

Is the reggae business really full of violence?

"It's better to know yourself if your record is a flop than to have someone else tell you. And if your record sells good the producer pretends he's gone to Nassau when you come by his office. In Jamaica, you're expected to use your machete, your knife, or your gun." JUNE, 1977

"What is there to benefit from badness? I wondered, looked at it and thought boy, bloodclaat, if I thump this man here, I feel the contact too. And then I said it's the same God that lives in my hand and that means it's not him I thump, it's God I'm really thumping." JULY, 1979

VIOLENCE

“The brethren are coming together, and we need a base away from police brutality and without disrespect from any people. Take Jamaica. Jamaica was in a great state of political violence, disturbances all over the place. But now the youth has seen it is no good so them come together in one harmony and fight no more.” FEBRUARY, 1978

“Me don't want fight no guy with no guns. Me mustn't fight for my rights, my rights must come to me. You stand up for your right and don't give up the fight, but you don't fight for your right.”

1975

Do you fear for your safety?

“No sah! Me nuh afraid fe dem. If I can avoid dem I avoid dem. If I'm going down the street and I see a road-block and there's a street for me to turn off before the road-block, ya better go and turn off. It's good not fe get search. NOW if somebody wan' kill I,

if somebody wan' try and hurt I, (other) than I and I make him hurt I, and if the only thing I can do is defend I-self, them I'm the one. I'm the one and let no-one on it. Rasta physical, ya know wha' I mean? We nuh come like no sheep in dem slaughter, like one time. Dem just don't have power fe do certain things to I and I. Dem just don't have it.”

MARCH, 1976

Lifestyle

"I don't eat meat, but it's easy, a Bible tell you what to do — mustn't eat pork, mule, horses, donkeys, duck, but you can eat fowl." JUNE, 1976

Do you drink?

"A little wine sometimes, that's all. Spirits (are) bad. Alcohol wrong. Herb does grow." JUNE, 1976

"Rum mosh up ya insides. Just kill ya, like the system." JUNE, 1976

"You travel with your Ital chef? Well, most of the time we find some hotel what have kitchen and dem things. But now we're thinking of getting one of those kitchens on wheels. But food is no problem. Man shall not live by bread alone y'know. So if we can get no food we stay without food. I can live without food for a period of time." SEPTEMBER, 1980

"I have a BMW. But only because BMW stands for Bob Marley and The Wailers, and not because I need an expensive car." 1977

"(I drive) a jeep. An old jeep, so nobody will say I'm driving a BMW any more. I couldn't stand that BMW, ha ha ha! BMW make pure trouble!" SEPTEMBER, 1980

BOB MARLEY *Talking*

BOB MARLEY *Talking*

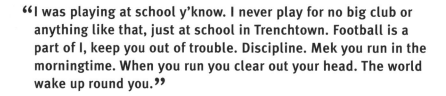

You play soccer?

"Yeh… I don't know my right position. Sometimes play defence, sometimes forward. I like to defend, but I like to attack too." **FEBRUARY, 1976**

"I was playing at school y'know. I never play for no big club or anything like that, just at school in Trenchtown. Football is a part of I, keep you out of trouble. Discipline. Mek you run in the morningtime. When you run you clear out your head. The world wake up round you."

Would you rather play football all the time than music?

"I love music before I love football. If I love football first maybe that a bit dangerous, because the football get very violent! I sing about peace and love and all of that stuff and something might happen, y'know. If a man tackle you hard it bring feelings o'war!"
AUGUST, 1980

"Plenty people have the wrong idea about this locks thing. Like I read in a magazine: 'Marley came onstage with his waxed locks'. Now that is very much a lie because I could never sit down and put wax on my hair, my wool, to keep it together. It would be clammy and stink man. Them blind man! This come natural."
JULY, 1975

"Anytime you can't laugh you're foolish: tension get you mash."
NOVEMBER, 1979

"Me love farming. Me wanna live 'pon a farm later. Me no really wanna live in a flat and go to a club every night and come back, and then do it again." APRIL, 1977

"Me is a planter by heart. Me grow up in it, y'know. That's the first thing me ever do—farming. Me grow up inna it and it is me really love. But the farming I used to do, it was slave farming with the machete and a hoe. Or we dig it by hand. We didn't have dem t'ing that you drive and plough it up." SEPTEMBER, 1980

❝My life here, this flesh; me have to live. Me never say there was no fear of death but me no deal with death. Me have no time to risk this flesh too much 'cause it's this me have to do it in.❞

NOVEMBER, 1979

❝At home I meditate and play music and play games: soccer, table tennis, draughts, Judo. But the greatest thing really is to get the physical together.❞ OCTOBER, 1976

❝If you didn't exercise in England when it rains then you wouldn't get much exercise at all.❞ APRIL, 1977

❝I am a man who deals by ear.❞ JUNE, 1976

❝It's a compulsion. I have to leave Jamaica certain time of year.❞ JULY, 1975

"My future is in a green part of the earth. Big enough me can roam freely. I don't feel Jamaica gonna be the right place because Jamaica look a bit small. That mean we put a circle some time round Jamaica, mean my thing will have finished, need somewhere new, Ethiopia, adventure, know what I mean?**"**

JULY, **1975**

"People out on the street, them ignorant, man! None of them really know how to live! Them should really know what is right and what is wrong." FEBRUARY, 1978

Do you hang out with other musicians?

"Me just hang out with I ownself.**"** JUNE, **1975**

"I only do creative work. Pure creative work." JUNE, 1975

"Me just a tighten up, is not really tense. If you laugh, laugh too much, everything just go in a little vain way. Somebody 'ave to tighten it up, 'ave to be like strict sometimes. And after the show we cool again.**"** JULY, **1975**

"When is music time, me serious. Just so me stay, we no in a joke business." JULY, 1975

LIFESTYLE

Women

"Who was that?" JUNE, 1977, AFTER BEING KISSED BACKSTAGE BY BIANCA JAGGER

Do you ever fall in love?

"Well, see, you mustn't give your strength to the woman. A woman is to be loved and appreciated. Woman is an earth, the mother of creation. Must love woman, but don't fall in love. Me stand in love. Love so much me look hungry. Pure love, dat. When you see me look vexed, dat 'cause me pucked a up with love." FEBRUARY, 1976

"Billie Holiday sings 'When your money done, you ain't got no friends'. If the money's done, you may not have a woman either!"
OCTOBER, 1975

"Children are wonderful. It don't take plenty y'know. Just a nice girl who don't take birth control. Sexual intercourse is a lovely thing." OCTOBER, 1975

"Me have four boys and three girls, and got one coming too. The eldest one is about eight, or seven." 1975

Do they like music?

"Yeah, them musicians. Them grow up and play music as a natural thing. Is righteousness, Jah will reward us. Children is wonderful, a part of my richness. Important to keep everything natural. If we live in truth, eat Ital food and love. Me never believe in marriage that much... marriage is a trap to control me; woman is a coward. Man (is) strong." JULY, 1975

RITA MARLEY

BOB MARLEY *Talking*

Do you admire any women?

"Dat woman in America... Angela Davis. A woman like that who defends something; me can appreciate that."

JULY, 1975

Female journalist:
"What will drinking Irish Moss do for me?"
"Wet your pumpum."

JANUARY, 1977

Are you planning to marry Cindy Breakespeare, Miss World?

"She's one of my girlfriends." APRIL, 1977

"Me nuh gamble y'know. Man in Jamaica say me a-win race horse. Me? I-man is a saint. My only vice is plenty women. Other that than, I-man is a saint to all dem accusation." APRIL, 1988

Herb

"The healing of a nation. Herb like fruit. Keep you healthy: mind clear." **JUNE, 1976**

How much do you smoke?

"Plenty." JUNE, 1976

"Devil make smoking illegal because Devil don't want people thinking one way. My friends feel the same as I when we smoke. We reach one another, y'know? Dat's what Babylon afraid of, that people all think the same." **JUNE, 1976**

"Why people drink is they want feeling I get when I smoke herb. Everybody need to get high but some people getting high with the wrong things." JUNE, 1976

"They took me in a room and searched me. The one guy was speaking in English and I could understand him, but the other guy was talking in German but I could pick up on the vibrations, and he kept saying "He must have it!" And they brought dogs and the whole trip but I didn't care because I didn't have any. We didn't come to break the German law. I didn't have any and I didn't need to have it because God guides and protects me and he won't let me go to jail." **1976, AFTER A POLICE RAID IN DUSSELDORF**

"Hey! Cops! Anybody got anything flush it, flush it!"

JUNE, 1977, FRANCO-BELGLAN BORDER

"Every time I come through the Customs I get likkle search. Them do according to things you carry with you. If you're carrying a small t'ing you get a small search, if you're carrying a big thing, about four or five hours. They saying 'Well, he must have something'." **AUGUST, 1980**

BOB MARLEY *Talking*

Any shortage of ganja in Jamaica?

"Dat's the only one dat place have plenty of, bwai. Plenty herb ! I prefer Lambsbread y'know, or Jerusalembread. Dat is something like cotton. We used to call it Goatshit. Strong herb, real good stuff." SEPTEMBER, 1980

You smoke herb in Zimbabwe?

"Yeh, one night we go to a soldier place and a guerilla call out to me and give me a touch of something... and that was it. No wonder they won the war! Tell ya bwai (boy), dem mon smoke some good herb mon! De tell me they smoke that herb and feel brave. Them tell me it make them... invisible." SEPTEMBER, 1980

"The more people smoke herb, the more Babylon fall."

FEBRUARY, 1976

"When you smoke herb it reveals you to yourself. All the wickedness you do is revealed by the herb—it's you conscience and gives you an honest picture of yourself." SEPTEMBER, 1980

"Maybe you could meditate without herb if you're somewhere that's quiet, but even if you go into the woods there's still the birds. But if you smoke herb the birds might sound sweeter and help you to meditate." 1978

"The authorities tell you that you mustn't smoke herb because it's bad for you. Yet if they catch you at it they'll carry you off to prison. I think it's better to be smoking herb out here free than being in prison." 1978

HERB

BOB MARLEY *Talking*

Stardom

As one of the most important figures that reggae has produced, do you feel a responsibility or even a nervousness?

"I don't even think of it, you know? If somebody don't say that to me I don't think about what's happening." JUNE, 1976

"I don't feel like it's a burden. Things don't get worse, ever. Things get better. No problem to me." JUNE, 1976

"My friends? They don't know what is happening—well, they know, but they am so COOL!" JUNE, 1976

"It makes no difference. I not hungry for anything before people internationally started singing my songs." JUNE, 1976

"Me no enjoy success y'know. Look 'ow slim me is. Me just come to do God's work, me no really enjoy it." JUNE, 1976

"Any man tell you. You ask anyone 'pon street who know me from long time. 'You know Bob?' 'From long time'. 'Do you see any changes?' 'He stay same all the while, never have nothing a change, he's just one man with the knowledge fe do things and accept the truth.'" MARCH, 1978

"No, I don't want success. Success is not 'in'. You follow they (their) system and the system kill ya." JUNE, 1976

"Money doesn't matter. Only music matters. When people think first about money and then about the music the music won't be worth the money they were thinking about." 1977

Has your career been a success?

"I've been always successful from beginning. It's like we come with success. We don't get success, we come with it. I am success myself. That is where success is." JUNE, 1975

How do you handle fame?

"I handle fame by not being famous... I'm not famous to me."
DECEMBER, 1974

"Monee, monee, can't spoil you. They mustn't let money spoil them. I'm not to see that plenty people do spoil at your money, because I still know me have good friends. Once money spoil you, boy, you ain't got no friends. You friends is your money—that mean that all the people we have around here, them like you because you have money—and then when your money done, you're finished. You have plenty people sing themselves, 'When you're money done, you ain't got no friends'." **1975**

"I learned. I learned from when I was coming in, from when I just start the music. People have warned me. They show me—hey, this game is a game where if your mind don't (isn't) sharp, you will lose your consciousness. The only way you will lose your consciousness is if you figure you are reh reh reh (boasting)... people say your head might swell. And if your head swell, that's it. So I just keep my head in a bandage that it cannot swell."

DECEMBER, 1974

"You find that most people, when they get money, they get withdrawn and foolish. Money is not my richness. My richness is to live and walk on the earth barefoot." **OCTOBER, 1975**

"I lived for a long time without money before I started to make money, but my work isn't aimed at becoming a star and I'm making sure my life don't go towards material vanity... I won't deny that at times I get a certain enjoyment out of success but it's worldly enjoyment and I don't need it because it destroys you." JUNE, 1976

"Me is a natural man like any other man, and me feel like any other man. Me nuh really feel like a entertainer or a star or any o'dem t'ing deh. Me know what me want, me know whey (where) me come from, and me know whey me go." **AUGUST, 1976**

Media

"Sometimes it nice fe get some promotion and really get the word out deh. Interview is a must, help me personally more than any other thing because most radio station don't play my music, just magazine people read (about it)." SEPTEMBER, 1975

"Some of what is written really good. Some of it really embarrassing. One thing I prefer is when the young guy ask questions (rather) than an old guy. An old guy don't understand, and not interested to know either. He's gone a little too far and you can't get him back... y'know, pension and all that!" JUNE, 1976

"Me no care what critics say; if me make a mistake me know me make a mistake." JUNE, 1975

CEDELLA, JULIAN, STEVE AND ZIGGY

BOB MARLEY *Talking*

"Plenty things wrong sometimes (in press interviews). The mistake me see them make is when them misinterpret what Rastafari really mean. And sometimes them talk about dreadlocks, head wax and all them things." SEPTEMBER, 1975

"Dese (these) newspapers don't understand, or they want to crush my thinking into the dust.**" 1978**

"Reggae music on radio mustn't deal as a programme for people to enjoy as a musical t'ing. It must be an educational programme. That means I want to look forward to hear something 'bout all mankind's struggle for life. It can't be 'OK, this is Bob Marley, this is John Holt, this is Dennis Brown'. You must have content in this package." 1975

"When I was living in Ghost Town, no writers came down there, you understand? When I was living in Ghost Town, leaning against all that zinc, with the burial ground right in front of me, there was nobody there. So we move uptown and the writers come.**"**

JULY, 1976

Illness

"In Paris I was playing soccer and a man gave me a raas-claat tackle in the rain. The foot started paining me and I wonder now why it kept burning for so long. Bwai, (boy) I score a goal and just hop off the field. When I took off my shoe, the toenail was completely out." 1977

"They don't want to run this thing like how I want to run it. Them want to run me on a star trip, but I realise my structure run down, I must rest. But they are not concerned with my structure. Dem run and plan a North American tour. I watch Muhammad Ali and Alan Cole (Jamaican footballer and member of Marley's entourage) and I see how these athletes take care of their structure. But the people who set up the tour do not work. Them just collect the money and when night come you find them in bed with two girls while you bus' your raas-claat and work all the time. When my toe was injured, they didn't even know my toe-nail had just come out and the bwai (boy) dem still set up a North American tour. They had planned to cut off my toe just so I could make the tour. 'Exodus' was a-bubble (starting to cause a stir) and if I make the tour 'Exodus' would sell over a million. His Majesty (Crown Prince Asfa Wossen, the son of Haile Selassie) said to me in London, 'Is what sin you do to agree to cut off your toe?' So I just say to them (businessmen), 'Fuck off and go away'. So I just decide and take a rest." 1977

BOB MARLEY *Talking*

" I got a pain in my throat and head and it's killing me. It's like somebody's trying to kill me. I feel like I've been poisoned. And something wrong with my voice. I've never felt like this before in my life. " AUGUST, 1980

" Hail Rasta! Ya t'ink anyt'ing can raas kill me? I understand that writers and people in the press are very interested and concerned about my health. I want to say thank you for your interest and that I'll be back on the road again in 1981 — really, performing for the fans we love. Beautiful y'know. It's Bob talkin' to ya, have no doubt, see? Good. " NOVEMBER, 1980

" Like so many other patients who have come here (Dr Josef Issels clinic, Bavaria), I was given up by the doctors to die. Now I know I can live. I have proved it. "

MARCH, 1981

" I've gone inside myself more. I have had time to explore my beliefs, and I am the stronger because of it. " MARCH, 1981

Natural Mystic

"I've been here before and will come again, but I'm not going this trip through." **1979**

"Music is a dangerous game. A musician man is a man him soft in him heart. Him slightly different." SEPTEMBER, 1975

"I don't know if I'm going to sound funny to you, but I really have no expectation in life. You know what I mean? Me always grow, and the things that I grow with, I never give them up. Like the trees, the sweet-smelling trees where you take 'em, boil tea and drink. Bush tea. I kyaan (can't) give up that which gives happiness. There's a lot of things me really love and money kyaan buy them tilings."
SEPTEMBER, 1980

How old are you?
"Today. About 30? No, I'm today. I come like the day. I don't really have a birth." FEBRUARY, 1976

"God created the earth for us, but people wonder, 'Who owns the tree? Who owns the ladder? Who owns the ganja pipe?" **JUNE, 1980**

"There are two roads. One is life and one is death. And if you live in death then you must be dead. And if you live in life you must live. The way the mouth say, make you live." FEBRUARY, 1976

BOB MARLEY *Talking*

"When the time comes, people will seek the truth in all things. They get it when they are ready to hear it." AUGUST, 1978

"When you rest at night-time you put your head down and go sleep. Where yourself is at dat time? Yet you awake again." FEBRUARY, 1976

"Me can't tell you the things dat will happen. Me just wait. Prophecy the last thing." FEBRUARY, 1976

"It's the last days without a doubt. 1975. It's the last quarter before the year 2000 and righteousness—the positive way of thinking—must win. Good over evil. We're confident of victory." JULY, 1975

"People don't get time to expand their intelligence. Sometimes I think the most intelligent people are the poorest —they just want to eat." JUNE, 1980

"The thing is you can't say 'the spirit' —I can only see what I see in front of me. So this is reality and the time is short 'cause you never can tell, a new breeze can blow." NOVEMBER, 1979

"If you're in the country at night... when the rain fall at night it's the best y'know, because all 'hear is the rain play music on the leaves." APRIL, 1977

"Life... it's life we deal with. No death. He that sees the light and knows the light shall live." MAY, 1973

"This is where people make a mistake. They say that the flesh doesn't value anything, but that's the biggest lie. The flesh is what you've got, what God put inside you is your life." JULY, 1979

ZIGGY AND CEDELLA

"Don't look on people as something else, look on people just as people. God's creations. I don't check the paper or check the book, I just go on feelings."

JUNE, 1976

"My head is not in the material world. I'm a man who sleeps on stone. Go into the hills and rest. That's my pleasure. I own the earth you know, all things belong to I." JUNE, 1974

"My home is what I think about. My home is not a material award out there somewhere y'know. My home is in my head."

AUGUST, 1976

"Bob Marley isn't my name. I don't even know my name yet."

JUNE, 1974

"Me look inside of me. Me hardly see outside, y'know. My eyes turn inside of me. Me don't care what people do or people say, me look for the right things you know." JUNE, 1975

"I'm into what I'm into now because I was born into what I'm into."

JUNE, 1975

"Me not of the world, y'know. Me live in the world but I'm not of the world." JUNE, 1975

"We need positive vibrations. 'Cause first thing you cannnot be ignorant, you have to be very intelligent. Want to cut the negative thing out entirely, negative, outside. Have to be positive. It's what your mouth say keep you alive. It's what your mouth say, kill you. And the greatest thing is life." JUNE, 1975

What's your rising sign?

"Well, me never know nothing 'bout that."

What's your moon sign?

"Me never know nothing 'bout that neither. Me just know some natural things." JUNE, 1975

"We're just children on the earth, but our mind all wiggy woggy (mixedup). No one teaching the real way of life, and right now the devil have plenty influence. But as far as me is concerned, all the Devil's influence lead to is death." JUNE, 1976

"Ya just a fe (have to) live right. The ship rock, but we still steady."
MARCH, 1976

"Man is a universe in himself." APRIL, 1988

"My music will go on forever. Maybe it's a fool say that, but when me know facts me can say facts. My music go on forever."
JUNE, 1975

NATURAL MYSTIC